MAGNIFIED THOUGHTS

For information contact: www.magnifyyouressence.wordpress.com

Book and Cover design by Carolyn Wilson

ISBN-13: 978-1976286001
ISBN-10: 197628600X

First Edition: September 2017

10 9 8 7 6 5 4 3 2 1

MAGNIFIED THOUGHTS

A Transformational Journey to Reveal Your Amazing You

CAROLYN WILSON

This book is dedicated to all survivors of sexual child abuse, domestic violence and any one who has lost a sense of self and seeking a way to be found. Know that you are incredible and that your thoughts have the power to set yourself free to reveal your amazing you !!!

Carolyn

When I discover who I am, I'll be free

- Ralph Ellison -

Carolyn Wilson

First and Foremost, giving Thanks and Praise to my Higher Power. God has a purpose & a plan for my life - Jeremiah 29:11

- ❖ I dedicate this book to my mother Barbara Wilson as she would have been extremely proud of me. She's my Angel. #918
- ❖ To my children who spent countless hours by my side. Thank you so much for understanding. Mommy loves you!
- ❖ To my rock solid support system – my family. I love you guys for always being there no matter what. #familyfirst
- ❖ To my Pastor and Church family who kept me lifted in prayer.
- ❖ To all my friends who walked along this journey with me. Thanks for listening, and your support.
- ❖ To all who stood with me in order to seek justice. I got through that time because of you. #ilovemyvillage
- ❖ To all survivors of sexual child abuse and domestic violence this is for you. #weareconquers

And most importantly to my little sister who unbeknownst to her essentially saved my life. Through God's divine timing we literally saved each other.

Foreword

I really like the layout and the format of the book. It's like a guidebook for the reader to create their own magnified thoughts. This is really innovative and I love that it's designed for personalization. I also like the fact that it's low-tech. No seriously. In a world of social media and screens and likes and notifications, I really like that this book gets people away from all of that so that they can just be with their pencil, this book, and their thoughts.

~ Russell Dinkins, Princeton University

Your thoughts become your words, your words
become your actions, your actions become your
character and at the end of the day your
character is who you become! ~ M.Y.E.

Magnify Your Essence

Introduction

Listed in this book you will find my words of expression through my creative writings and quotes that I used to stay motivated. It is my hope that my thoughts will resonate with someone to uplift one's spirit, to get one moving and to just think differently. Quotes and positive affirmations are soothing to my soul and I wanted to share my thoughts as something inspired me. Personally, I live by quotes. They may be short and sweet but packed with a lot of ah-ha moments. These are some of the quotes I published during the first year of my journey while discovering self and starting Magnify Your Essence along with Women on the Move - Power Hour a few years ago. Both of which have become a phenomena in its own right by inspiring hundreds of women and men who attended my empowerment seminars. And, thousands have been reached all around the world by way of my simple yet powerful what I like to call my "little chia pet blog". (Because, my blog is just like a chia pet you set it, wait and watch it grow.) I absolutely love these post and quotes as they tell a story as to where I was with my thoughts and how I want others to be. Positivity is a choice! You can accepted it or reject it. In my life, in my journey I chose not only to accept it but to embrace it. I hope you can find some comfort and motivation in some of my post and quotes best know my TDN - (Today's Daily Nugget). This is because as I walk through my journey, I am intentionally leaving little nuggets for others to pick up along the way. Enjoy! Be Empowered! Be Inspired! Be Magnified!

CONTENTS

Understanding

Relax, Relate, Reminisce about where
you've been, where you're at, and where
you are yet to go! Embrace It! ~ M.Y.E.

Magnify Your Essence

In order for you to understand the significance of the Magnified Thoughts in this book you must first understand the significance of my story, my journey and how they all came together to be transformational to me.

For years, I existed only to merely exist. I was on autopilot just going about life without a sense of direction, a sense of guidance, or a sense of purpose. I was truly unclear on who I was and what I was meant to do in this life. I didn't understand my value or my worth. Life had placed quite a few obstacles in my way that ordinarily would stop a person in their tracks –mentally, physically and spiritually. Obstacles that would make some choose to cease their existence instead of dealing with the emotional and physical difficulty of these unfortunate circumstances.

As a young child I was molested by my father until I was a teenager. *I felt unloved.* I was diagnosed with Scoliosis requiring major spinal surgery. *I felt different.* I became a teenage mother. I was on welfare. *I felt embarrassed.* I lost my mother in my late twenties. *I felt alone.* I was involved in 2 abusive and controlling relationships. *I felt isolated.* I spend years in court related to criminal stay away orders, PFA (protection from abuse) orders, and custody and child-support cases. *I felt depleted.* I had low self-esteem. I became severely depressed. *I felt unworthy.* I had completely lost myself and who I was to the point where my own mirrored image was unrecognizable. *I felt invisible.*

But God! But only by the grace of God, I was able to still press forward and accomplish great things in spite of all those mishaps. Fortunately, I was able to raise a son who is now an alumnus of Princeton University. I was able to return to college and earn 3 degrees. I have served on many non-profits boards of directors and have held executive leadership roles to name a few of the many seemingly impossible accomplishments based upon my background.

In the midst of accomplishing those feats there was always a sense of not feeling worthy of achieving any of it. I felt as if I was trapped between two worlds by being a part of both but not belonging to either. Being on autopilot is essentially how I maneuvered through life. However, I always felt like there was something more to my life and something was missing but I couldn't quite place my finger on it.

It has always been important for me to keep the faith and have a positive outlook on things even when it was hard for me to believe my own thoughts. But in essence it was my own thoughts that was keeping me from my own greatness.

My thoughts were that I always sensed there was a disconnection in my life from who I was truly supposed to be. I made myself believe that my light never burned or shined brightly even though I knew that it should. Nothing in my life ever seemed right. It was my thoughts that was keeping me extremely unsettled.

This was my reality until a spark within me was ignited in 2012 when I thought about how I could put the pieces together and make sense of my life. I knew the what, but didn't quite know the how. In 2013, an event occurred that catapulted that spark into what seemed to me as being a cataclysmic explosion. This was the event that changed everything for me, this was my how. As this event made me revisit my past. It made me face my deepest fears. It made me unearth what had been buried. It made me deal with the sexual abuse, the molestation that I endured as a young child and as a teenager. It made me have to come face to face with my perpetrator, the man I called daddy…my father. It made me discover what I truly was all along – Strong!

This explosive event started to burn purpose into my life as the flames got stronger so did I. And, in 2014 that fire burned to create a passion that revealed who I truly was and what I was meant to do. Out of the ashes my true purpose and meaning to my life was birthed – Magnify Your Essence. Magnify means to increase or enlarge and Essence means your soul, your being who you are. Because of the fire, and what God said in Jeremiah 29:11, plans to prosper, not harm, plans for hope and a future, my Essence has been Magnified!

The quote that resonated with me the most at that time was from Ralph Ellison – which states *"When I discover who I am, I'll be free"*. I finally became free. I no longer had thoughts to keep me from my greatness. Rather my thoughts propelled me into my greatness. I had revealed how amazing I was. I completely mastered the power of positive thinking. This complete mindset shift in my thinking was so profound that it became infectious to others around me.
My thoughts became my Magnified Thoughts to keep me grounded to keep me pushing, and to keep moving forward. I became so excited about this transformation that I wanted others to experience this journey and have a total transformation for themselves.

Because of this journey many individuals, women and even men have been impacted in a positive way by the following initiatives I created and implemented: my blog turned ministry – Magnify Your Essence; Women on the Move - Power Hour Empowerment Seminars & Workshops; 30-day Water Challenge; Beacon's Light Women's Retreat; Celebrating YOU Women's Conference & Expo and my daily quotes known as TDN (Today's Daily Nuggets). All these platforms and initiatives were created in order to foster a can do attitude and a positive atmosphere that inspires and motivates others.

This journey has not only allowed me to transform my life from just existing to completely living but has allowed me to share this remarkable journey with others all so they can discover their true self, be Magnified and be Fearlessly Free.

The pages in this book will guide you towards changing your thoughts and your way of thinking. Each blog post and quote has meaning and purpose to uplift your spirit. Reflect on each section "Magnified Thoughts" & "Magnified Quotes" as you read through this book. You might want to bookmark thoughts that speak directly to you. After the post section and after each quote you can write how these thoughts apply to you. Write down what comes to mind. Then make it your own. Embrace it…Believe it…Become it!

This is the beginning towards your total mindset shift and your own magnified thoughts. Take this book and keep it with you wherever you go as a reminder that the power of positive thinking lies between you, your beliefs and your thoughts.

Let me leave you with my own personal motto that I thought before, during, and after my transformation that still holds true to this day - "*I believe that self-determination through any circumstances leads to prosperity. If you can see it, and you believe it, you can achieve it. Just simply speak 'it' into existence and 'it' will be yours when the time is right.*" ~ Carolyn Wilson.

My Thoughts

(My Magnified Thoughts)

Overall the next several pages you will find a select few of my favorite blog posts that definitely helped me navigate through my journey. Although, written to motivate and encourage me, I believe they were truly written with you in mind. At the end of this section take a moment to write your own magnified thoughts that will inspire you.

If not Now, then When

"If not now…then when" is a phrase I would often hear but not fully embrace it until now. Thirty days ago I decided to be valiant. I decided to follow my hearts desires and step out on faith. I decided to let go of any inhibitions and just do "IT". So what is "IT" you might ask? Well, "IT" is to be a beacon for others, to motivate, to inspire, and to empower those who cross my path. I want to be a genuine resource for all but especially for women in every walk of life that anything is possible.

Through my life experiences and journey, I want to be a living example for others to emulate. My journey has had its share of many obstacles and hindrances that would normally stop a person in their tracks and keep them right where they stand. So many that statistically my life should have had a much different outcome. But, I am proud to say that through my faith, my resilience, and my determination I have transcended and surpassed all these barriers. I have learned and I'm still learning many lessons along my life's passage. I have realized the secret to my existence and I know that I am living an abundant and fulfilling life contrary to these statistics.

I just want the same for others…for each person to reach their potential, to know their own worth, to be happy with oneself. Then to pass it on…each one teach one I always say. It's astonishing that somehow I've always been the one to help people in some way shape or form. The one whom people sought and respected my opinion and guidance. It has been something that came so natural and was effortless that I never realized helping others is what brought me pure joy.

This is my gift…this is my passion…this is my purpose. I am bringing "IT" to fruition what has innately already been there. Once I have discovered my true self the doors and windows to endless possibilities have opened for me. Because I know who I am and what I want I've become even more resilient, fearless, and determined to let go and be me.

My dream of being someone who's influential and an agent of change is now my reality. This experience is what brought about this blog….magnify your essence. This concept, this idea, this way of life…the journey to discovering the true you will manifest greatness for all. This will be the stepping stone to greater things. My essence has been magnified and I want yours to be too!

This was the beginning of it all. I was scared to start this blog, but I decided to do it anyway. Just think if I didn't. Thank God I did. The launch of Magnify Your Essence - April 18, 2014

Life's Gaper Delays

Have you ever been on the highway cruising going at nice pace, you're making good timing, the road is all clear, and you're on target to reach your destination? All this makes you feel good, free and relaxed because all the signs lead to great travels. Until, all of a sudden you start to slow down and that once clear road has turned into bumper to bumper traffic creeping, almost as if traffic were not moving at all, but rather standing still.

Now that great feeling is replaced with frustration, anxiety, and wonderment. What happened?!? What is going on?!? Will you ever get there?!? You were on track and now this something unknown has halted your progress.

How baffling is this that you have no idea how things could all of a sudden can go so off the mark. You have places to go, people to see and people awaiting your arrival. During this time you question your every move. Should you have left earlier, drove a little faster, or took a different route?

You also are looking at the other side of the road in awe that they are moving and going somewhere while you're left standing still. There is no fun in seeing others move and whiz right by you especially when you know you have somewhere to be but feel like you're losing valuable ground. All of which are reasonable thoughts, but at this point irrelevant, because you are the one who's still stuck and dormant.

Then only after some time has passed, just as soon as you stopped in a split second you start to move once again. As you're driving by the area of uncertainty, you curiously look to see what in world impeded your movement in the first place. Sometimes it's something in your direct path or it's something on the other side of the road. It could be a road block, an accident, a random piece of debris or sometimes there's nothing at all that makes any sense to have caused such a Gaper Delay.

Either way, you gain some clarity as to what it was or wasn't and then you start to regain your momentum. You're now right back on track, cruising down the highway, still on target to reach your destination with or without some minor adjustments and feeling good once more again.

In life, we will definitely have Gaper's delays, traffic jams, and other obstacles that will hinder us. These things will prevent us from moving forward towards our goals and aspirations. But, know that when this happens it's not the setback that stands out but it's that precise moment of clarity is when you realize what has happen. That's the second you regain momentum. You become recharged and even more determined to reach your purpose that you were greatly destined for. Remember…Delays are inevitable but clarity is unmistakable.

Pushing Past Your Limits

What are limits? Who sets them? Limits are defined as the final, utmost or furthest boundary or point. Knowing this definition one might question, who actually sets these limits? Who sets them on ourselves? Who sets the "final point" or "boundary" on anything that we do? Good question, right? Well don't be surprised by the answer. It's you!

If I had to guess, I would estimate we do this at least 80% of the time if not more. You are the one setting your own boundaries, ending point, and determine your own limits. We tell ourselves what we can and cannot do all of the time. We put limits on our own abilities to be and do greater things. After all, it is okay to know your own limits but it's not okay when we live and exist beneath them.

In order to be great we must do great things. In order to be great we must dare to be great. We do this by putting our limits to the test and push beyond how far we imagine our limits can go. If you don't challenge your limits you'll never know how great you can be.

Take for instance an athlete, they know what they are and not capable of doing. They only get better when they push past their own boundaries. They have removed the limits and have allowed themselves to be open to limitless possibilities. The greatest athletes have set themselves apart from the rest because there are no boundaries hindering their progress.

This is what we must do with ourselves, live a limitless life by releasing the boundaries that confine us. When this happens we will then rise to a greater version of ourselves. Pushing past your limits simply means you have to P.U.S.H. (Persist - Until - Something - Happens) for infinite possibilities exist within you!

True Happiness Begins with Me!

On this day, I celebrate me! I celebrate all that I have accomplished and all that is still yet to do. I celebrate all that I am and all that I will be! You see happiness is the key to everything in this lifetime. When things are going well in your life it can be attributed to simply being happy. So what is being happy exactly?

According to Merriam-Webster, there are three distinct definitions for the word happy.

adjective \ˈha-pē\
: feeling pleasure and enjoyment because of your life, situation, etc.
: showing or causing feelings of pleasure and enjoyment
: pleased or glad about a particular situation, event, etc.

And, the word happiness is defined as the state of being happy.

So since being happy is simply a state of being, why choose to be anything else but that? I know this is what I choose and the benefits far out way any other feeling. Take for instance, there was a time in my life where I was stuck and depressed about my life and how it had come to what it did despite all my accomplishments.

During this dark time, I wasn't happy and the residual effect of this made me stressed; which in turn made me sick; gain too much weight and generally stop caring about me. All the above, definitely didn't contribute to me being blissful. I was far from it. However, in time I realized that I am in control of my own state of being, my happiness was determined by me.

Gradually, I began to feel and be less stressed; I no longer had physical symptoms of my mystery illness; I gradually began to lose the extra weight; and I started to care about me. I would have people ask me all the time what did I do to lose weight and I would boldly state "I'm Happy!" Pharrell was on to something when he made that catchy "Happy" song. It definitely has some truth to it and it sure makes you feel cheerful. At least, it does for me every time I hear it.

Because now that I am happy, I have become more resilient, I have become more confident, I have become free to be myself, therefore, I am more in tune with me. I do want to acknowledge that there are people and things that do add to my happiness. I place a strong emphasis on the part "add to" because that's their only source.

I am the cause of my happiness simply because of me first! I allow myself to feel pleasure and enjoyment because of my life. For that reason, my true happiness begins with me and I am truly happy!

The Art of Letting Go

Letting go sounds easier than one thinks. But it contradicts everything we have ever been told. In preschool, we are taught to grab our friends hand and don't let go when on a trip or walk to the park. When crossing the street your mother or guardian said "hold my hand and don't let go". When you first rode the merry-go-round and sat on the moving horse you were told to "hold on and don't let go". When you were given a balloon you were told to "hold it tight and don't it let go".

Sometimes we were even physically tied to or buckled in to the very things we were told not to let go of. So, no wonder we have a hard time letting things go. It has been ingrained in us since as long as we can remember to hold on and don't let go.

Well, now it is time to let go! Letting go is an act of freeing oneself from something. You stand alone and not in unison with something that ties you down. Although, the mere thought of this can be frightening it is alright to let go. Take for instance what happens to you and the balloon when it gets released.

As a child, you may be upset about the loss of something that was once connected to you; something you loved, adored or even cherished. You lost it because you didn't hold on tight like you normally do. Now, if we look at what the balloon does as it leaves us, it flies away and ascends as far as we can see. It keeps going until it ultimately becomes a distant memory.

You eventually get it together and then move on despite just loosing what you thought was so important to you. So now, the loss of the balloon doesn't affect you anymore because it is no longer present, it is simply gone.

The balloon represents the things in your life that you must learn to let go. You must release these things, people, feelings, situations, circumstances or even something about yourself. When you hold on to these tangible and intangible things you are bound and tied to them and take them everywhere you go.

Most of the things you hold on too are not good for your overall well-being and spirit. It becomes a constant reminder of its hindrance on your life and prevents you from moving forward. But when you learn to let these things go just like the balloon you are set free and that is the most liberating moment that any person can have.

You become unbound from all the things that has kept you tied and connected. It is time to let go. So, contrary to what you have been taught since as far back as you can remember it is so okay to let go for the betterment of you. Once you have learned and mastered the "art of letting go" the real beauty of this masterpiece is where your life's journey and true healing begins. So go ahead release those balloons in your life, let them fly but watch you soar!

Move Beyond Your FEAR!

The word fear has many meanings all of which pertains to being afraid. It is an emotion that one feels when you are in distress. According to Psychology Today, fear is a vital response to physical and emotional danger – Traumas or bad experiences can trigger a fear response within us that is hard to quell. [1] Fear makes us automatically go into protection mode when we are fearful of something or someone.

We hide, we avoid, we protect, and we often disregard the reality that is in front of us and panic about the situation. Because of this, we often give life to what we fear the most.

In my opinion, Fear is something that we often create. We tell ourselves what we should and shouldn't be afraid of. I heard this saying once from Rev. Beard in a sermon that Fear is nothing more than False Evidence Appearing Real. Therefore, I take it as it just doesn't exist. Fear is what YOU make it.

I was in the diner as I was putting together this post and I turned to the two beautiful seasoned women behind me and simply asked them...what does fear mean to them? You see I've learned with age comes wisdom and I wanted to get their perspective on this subject. Both unanimously responded "it's the unknown". One said, "It is something that you anticipate, the torment you put yourself through when you do not know". "Also, we should not lean to your own understanding and should trust in the Lord", she boldly stated. "It's all in our mind", the other one expressed. But they both agreed that fear can only be present if you let it.

Wow, I was on the right track with my thought process. They basically confirmed, this notion of fear not existing and that we ultimately create it. How true that is when I think of things within my own life that has caused me great distress and what I believed I was fearful of. Sometimes it was people but mostly it was situations or things that I really had control over but I let fear set in and take over.

The other day, I was looking through one of my old journals and I came across this statement that I wrote:

What is FEAR to me…?

F – Forever in bondage

E – Exiled from the world

A – Ashamed to speak & Acknowledge the past

R – Resentment of self & Resistant to a better life

I wrote this at a time when I was trying to figure out my life and why I wasn't able to move forward. The fact of the matter is I actually was making great moves. However, the fear I had lingering around felt as if I was going up on the down escalator…moving but going nowhere at the same time. You see at that time I acknowledged that I was allowing FEAR to keep me still and in place. This was the beginning of a new start and a new way of thinking for me.

A way to move beyond the fear that was holding me hostage. A way to no longer stay hidden from those around me. A way to talk about and accept my past. A way to love myself and embrace my enriched life. The way I moved beyond my fears was to move beyond all things that simply didn't exist.

Remember it is merely False Evidence Appearing Real. You too can also Move Beyond your FEAR by not giving it a permanent residence in your life. So with that in mind, stamp it return to sender because FEAR no longer lives here!

No More Doubt... You have a Purpose!'

I have been contemplating on my next post for quite some time now. The reoccurring theme of DOUBT kept coming up because in my own present life, I was becoming doubtful of this blog, of my Power Hours, of my conference, and of my everything. So, I knew this had to be the next entry because just like me so many others are plagued with the dreaded "D" word DOUBT.

It amazed me how one can be bold, be fearless yet still have room to be doubtful. I had to acknowledge that there is no room for any uncertainty if I am to proceed with the task put before me. The task that I have come to embrace as my talent, gift and purpose. In order to be even bolder and more fearless, doubt had to be removed and take a back seat. Just as fear once did along with holding on and letting go.

You see all of this transformation is a process...one that takes time, patience and the belief in the yet unseen or unknown. Each time something gets removed you are no longer chained and you become free. You then add to your boldness and fearless attitude way of life. Doors begin to open and more possibilities for you are soon revealed.

Take for instance with my "what am I doing" party, the question I often asked myself when the "D" word would manifest. I would start getting reassurance that all is well and to stay on the course. I knew I wanted to write about this thing called DOUBT but didn't know how or what I was going to say about it.

That is until now, as I lay across the bed while at a Christian Retreat Center in upstate New Jersey. I came up here to spend the day with some fellow retreaters before heading back home. My plan was to go up and drive right back the same day. A drive that should have taken me 1 ½ took me over 3 hours to get to the retreat center. I was thinking the entire time am I crazy to drive up there this late in the day 7 pm to only have to turn right back around in a few hours after I arrive.

However, I felt like I still needed to go even if it was for a couple of hours it would be more than worth it. Little did I know I would be handed a key to a room and given a place to stay. I was so appreciative of this offer because it was late and I was getting tired. I needed to rest especially since I was up all night the night before preparing for the conference. But, wait if you think that was amazing wait until I tell you this.

As I open the door to my quaint little room at the Christian Retreat Center, I am greeted by this sign on the desk which read "Be still and know I am God". Then the next thing I saw was a picture on the wall that read, "The joy of the Lord is your strength". I am in awe because these two sayings made complete sense to me.

I fell in love with this little retreat room because it was meant just for me. As I got ready for bed I noticed a little book that I thought was a bible but in fact it was actually one of those daily message books. So as I open the pages to try and locate the current date these are the three messages that appeared where the pages randomly stopped at...Blessing God in Adversity, Doubt & Victory through yielding. Wait!!!! What just happened here? These pages came up in this exact order, I was in pure amazement. My, my my...BUT GOD!

This is my message, this is my assurance that doubt needs to go. This is my post!!! This is the answer to what I've been seeking. The answer has been provided to me in a last minute, late night drive, to a retreat center, to a room, to a message left for me to give to you. Wow! Amazing right?

After this, I had to find the actual message for today's date and it was "The second rest". Hmm, so what is that? Well, it basically said when we go to HIM – He gives us rest. But, we often miss the second rest because we don't follow the directions or instructions given to us. Just like going to a doctor when we are sick but we don't follow the regiment prescribed to us to get completely better. When this happens we miss our second rest. So what I gather is that if we move beyond adversity through God's Blessing and move beyond DOUBT...we can receive victory through yielding based on the directions provided to us. Then we can reach our second rest. Make sense?

When we DOUBT we miss out on ALL our blessings. I know I almost did. The last picture that surrounded me in this room that at first didn't make sense to me until now read, "In me you may have peace, in this world you will have trouble, but take heart I have overcome the world".

I don't know about you but I know I completely felt the presence of my higher power – GOD – in that room. There was a purposeful flow to the messages that presented themselves. Clearly these messages were just for me to have no doubt.

I felt a sense of victory all because I yielded. So ask yourself are you yielding? Are you paying attention to the messages left just for you? If not, have no more doubt...because know that you do have a purpose. Your prescription has been written out...you just need to follow it as prescribed. Your purpose is waiting!

The Providential Compass

If one were to ask a basic question about what makes a compass work or what is it for? The simple answer would be a compass generally works by the earth's magnetic pull to always point to the North. Also, a compass is often used for navigation to provide guidance and direction to find a location. We use compasses all the time in the form of GPS in our cars or on our phones to provide us guidance and direction to get us to a particular place. But, when do we follow the guidance and direction of GOD or whatever you claim as your higher power to be?

I would say not often or not often enough. Mainly, because we don't listen or pay attention to the directions, signs or magnetic pulls that are given to us on a daily basis. I must admit, that I too was guilty of not listening or paying attention merely because of aimlessly wandering without a sense of direction or purpose. But, there comes a time for everyone when eventually something will grab your attention and jump out at you like a bright neon construction sign.

The reason for this is to get your immediate attention so you can follow the directions given. When you do so, this is when you start moving in the direction of your purpose. Essentially, your purpose starts to guide you and takes you places destined for you. If you closely pay attention to the destinations on your journey, you will start to see the connection that they each have. You will start to not only pay attention but will then be open to listen for further direction and guidance.

Just as you listen for the GPS to tell you to turn left or turn right. God is also ordering your steps and telling you the present and future direction in which you need to go, the places you need to be and the people you need to see. Have you ever had a time where you said, Wow…what a coincidence or it's happenstance that conveniently brought you to a particular place to run into a particular person. Coincidence…No…Providence…Yes.

I believe things happen all in according to God's Plan and for your purpose. Take for instance, my journey who would have thought I would be where I am now with this blog, with the workshops, with the women's empowerment conference, the places I've been, the people I've met and everything else that comes along with it. Well, not me that's for sure. I wouldn't have even imagined this is where I would be.

But, I am because overtime, I have learned to listen and follow the providential compass that has a magnetic pull on me and points me in the right direction. The direction that propels me further into my divined purpose. Even when it doesn't make the most sense to me, I know that it's favored.

I have simply learned to trust the route because guaranteed there will be something along the way that is purposed just for me. Each one of us has been given a special providential compass, a compass that comes with divine foresight to get you where you want and need to be in your life. Your compass is divinely designed to take you there and beyond.

All you have to do is trust what you hear (that inner voice), trust what you feel (that nudge or sense of well-being) and trust what you see (that of what you attract). Also, believe that everywhere you go, everything you do and everyone you encounter is predestined for your own greatness. So in knowing that, you must take hold of your providential compass…pay attention, listen carefully and pursue your destiny!!!

All When You Believe...

Miracles what are they? When do they occur? Well, miracles can be defined as a surprising and welcome event that is not explicable by natural or scientific law and is therefore considered to be the work of a divine agency according to a dictionary reference. Another way to look at miracles would be to consider them as an act from God. Usually, when they happen you are left in awe and pure amazement of the events that took place that seemed nearly impossible.

When thinking of miracles, I do know that they come when you least expect them but the key is you have to be able to believe that they are possible. This makes me think of the lyrics sung by Mariah Carey and the late Whitney Houston...

"There can be miracles when you believe... Who knows what miracles you can achieve when you believe, somehow you will when you believe"

Believing is the key to all things conceivable. Just think of a time when you did something out of the ordinary or something presented itself that worked in your favor that was unexplainable. So much that you were left scratching your head in wonderment of how it could be. All the while, being thrilled that the occurrence took place and manifested into what it did.

During either of these times you knew it was literally impossible for them to come about without some sort of divine intervention. But you believed it would and it did. Sometimes just your belief in something is merely enough to put things in motion. Simply put…whatever you think about, you bring about. Your thoughts become things that are beyond your control and will come to fruition.

Take for instance this way of thinking can be found in many places throughout the bible. One place in particular would be in Isaiah 55:11, where it says, "So is my word that goes out from my mouth: It will not return to me empty, but will accomplish what I desire and achieve the purpose for which I sent it."

It is stating that you speak things into existence that you believe. When times seems hopeless just remember these three key components: speaking, seeing and believing. When all of these are in play miracles do happen. And when they do, they happen at the right time and at the right moment. All you have to do is believe in what you believe then watch your miracles unfold!

B is for Breathing...

I have a quote book that I often have my students' reference to at the beginning of each class. Periodically, this one particular quote resurfaces…"we need the rocks in the road" which always sparks a discussion as to why we need them because to them it seems pointless. However, the common theme that comes up during our conversation is that during our journey we are sure to be faced with obstacles along the way.

These hindrance are our rocks. The rocks that will appear out of nowhere to prohibit you from moving forward. That is if you allow them too. The rocks in the road gives us the opportunity to be creative, to be resilient, to be determined, to continue and to move on. Let's face it rocks aren't always going to be in our way but when they do come it is how we handle them that will dictate the outcome of the perceived obstacle.

Take for instance earlier this month I had plans for an event. The location was set, notification of the event went out, the guest speaker confirmed, the materials printed, refreshments purchased, everything was a go at least, that's what I thought. When I arrived at the location an hour prior the event the doors were locked with a sign posted that the building had an emergency.

Talk about a rock in the road that was more like a huge boulder placed right smack in front of me. Seemed inevitable that the event was going to be cancelled. But, due to my tenacity the event still went on as planned.

Now normally when faced with an obstacle the normal reaction would be to ask what do you do? You have a choice to get angry, to panic, to give up or find another way. In this instance, I found another way how because there was a will and a desire not to give up.

I was asked to explain what I did in case someone was faced with a challenge that seems nearly impossible. What a great question to ask and what I came up with was that I never gave up. I didn't allow no for an answer. I did not panic nor complain.

What I practiced and the steps I took was something that I like to call *SELA (Stop, Evaluate, Listen, and Act)*. Take a moment to *STOP* complaining as it doesn't get you anywhere. You think about the facts and *EVALUATE* what you could and could not control in the situation. Be still and *LISTEN* for the answer in the calmness as that's when the answer will come to you. Then *ACT* on the possibility of another outcome.

When you practice *SELA* determination, faith, hope and persistence carries you through. This is what I did to come up with an alternative solution to my dilemma. This is the process I work through whenever I am faced with rocks in the road. It allows me to be creative, determined, and resilient to keep moving and to carry on. Ironically the word *SELA* in Hebrew means Rock and spelled with an "H" SELAH has a meaning of "to pause and think" how appropriate. So when obstacles come your way remember B is for Breathing, remove the rocks and just *SELA*!!!!

Actions Speak Louder Than Words...

Gratitude is something that in my opinion most take for granted and don't fully understand what it truly means. According to the actual definition of gratitude it means…the quality of being thankful; readiness to show appreciation for and to return kindness. The word gratitude is a noun which refers to a person, place or thing.

Well gratitude is this "thing" that is misunderstood. When you think about it the definition in itself has action that has to be taken in order for gratitude to be applicable. Hmm, then why is it not a verb. If we focused on the act of gratitude opposed to just being grateful we would soon realize you can't have one without the other.

You cannot feel grateful if you haven't taken any action to show it. Take for instance, I am thankful to my neighbors when they periodically cut my grass, shovel a path of snow or return my trash container from the curb. All simple gestures and I can say "thank you". But, am I truly grateful for their kindness?

Now most people just stop at saying thank you which technically is being grateful for their kindness. But, the next part is showing your gratitude by returning the kindness as the definition states. The act of my gratitude is showed when I do something in return. When this happens I am truly grateful and my gratitude is now complete.

It may not seem like it but there really is a difference when the action of gratitude is the focus opposed to just being. This is the best form of appreciation you will ever feel. There is a saying that Gratitude is the best Attitude, which simply means people who are grateful are the happiest and they attract more happiness into their lives.

Trust me when I say the act of being grateful changes everything. It did for me. So go ahead and show just how grateful you really are.

TRUST the P.R.O.C.E.S.S.

In the journey of self-discovery, we often want many great things for our life. When faced with something new instead of running from it or discrediting it. You should just let it flow and trust the process?

Hmm, so what is this exactly? And, how exactly do you do it? Trust that is...I mean, I don't know about you but the word TRUST has been unsettling for me for quite some time. This is such a small word but yet has such a big meaning and hold on most people including me.

So, what is this word anyway? What does it really mean? Well, according to dictionary.com the word trust has two distinct definitions one as a noun and the other as a verb. They are as follows:

noun: trust
firm belief in the reliability, truth, ability, or strength of someone or something.

verb: trust;
believe in the reliability, truth, ability, or strength of someone or something.

Based upon the definitions, I can personally admit I have had a belief in this thing called trust in its abstract form. However, it's the believing that has been the issue. You see whenever there is a verb involved it requires action and it must come directly from you.

So how can you have a trust but not act upon a trust? That is easy…because you can have a belief in someone or something but not believe. In order to believe one must actively have faith, assurance, conviction, and reliance with their entire being and whole heart. If you do not actively do these things then trust will not be there.

The reason why the trust may not be there in the first place is because for whatever reason you stop believing. More than likely an occurrence happened in your life that keeps you from believing in the reliability, truth, ability, or strength of someone or something.

However, this thinking can be undone. The reason why I know this is because this is where I am within my own journey. I have discovered that learning to trust is a process that takes place only after you have let go, forgave and have a sense of self-assurance. When you can allow yourself to act in this manner it is the ultimate form of vulnerability you can have for yourself. When this happens trusting no longer becomes a foreign unrealistic thing. I know I am learning to trust again because I now can believe.

So if you want to have all the things hoped for such as happiness, guidance, peace and love one must learn to trust the process. The process of being *Positive – Reasonable – Open-minded – Confident – Enthusiastic – Sincere – & – Strong* about what you want to believe is true and that is to be able to finally Trust.

Magnified Blessings

When I think of Blessings I think of the many saying and quotes about blessings and just being blessed. Such as "count your blessings count them one by one...count your blessings see what God has done" I think we have all sang that song a time or two. Other familiar sayings are "too blessed to be stressed" and "When Praises go up...Blessings come down". Once again, I'm pretty sure we had a personal connection with at least one of those sayings.

I see it as Blessings are those things that come when you least expect them. They are the things that you need the most. They are the things that help you to grow. They are the things that satisfies your hearts desires. Sometimes the things can be a person, a circumstance, or a situation, it's basically something that God sends just for you.

However, many people don't even realize that they are blessed. Because of this they often miss the true intentions of their blessings. Why? Well because they don't recognized them. You are truly blessed...beyond blessed when you become more in tune with your blessings and that just comes simply by recognizing them when they come.

When things happen to you or when people come into your life whether it be for a reason or a season it is a blessing. Sometimes it may not seem that way. But, truthfully speaking everything is a blessing. Everything goes in accordance to what is destined for you. There is always an underlining lesson for you to learn and grow from. Nothing is ever a coincidence or that things just happen.

Everything that happens to us, through us and around us are God's Blessings his Providence for us. This isn't just what I have come to believe, this is what I have come to know. I can say that the more I acknowledge and embrace my blessings the more blessings I know I will receive. I recognized that every situation, every circumstance, and every person that comes into my life has a purpose, a divine purpose.

These are not just blessings they are my Magnified Blessings and for that I'm thankful for each and every one of them. I can count them one by one and I can recognize them when they come. Can you? Do you recognized your blessings? What are YOUR Magnified Blessings?

Be Guided...

Have you ever had a time or moment in your life where things just seemed unclear? You just felt lost and unsure about what each day would bring? Well, guess what you are not alone. I remember feeling discombobulated so many times whereas I often wondered and asked WHY? Why me? Why is this happening? Why am I here? Why is it like this? Why is it like that? Why can't things be better? Why? Why? Why? Is what I often asked.

I remember being so entangled in my confusion that nothing made sense. Being pulled in so many different directions at the same time making it extremely difficult to see anything other than my own misery. To make matters worse the only thing that made sense was seeing that my own life was in shambles with all the signs pointing and validating yet more calamity.

For me these were definitely tough times. Times when I wanted to just give up. Times when I had lost all hope. Times of most certain despair. Times when I just couldn't take what life dished out. In those moments everything seemed so bleak, I felt so alone, so misunderstood and I was barely existing to exist. But by the grace of GOD, times are no longer bleak. The directions are much clearer now. I now know that I was not alone but others have felt this way at some point in their lives too. I also know that seeing their examples of pushing through helped me to get through as well.

I now know that those moments were necessary for my unveiling of a new polished me. Just like a broken ragged piece of glass that gets weathered and tossed about in the ocean waters, overtime becomes this smooth uniquely stunning piece of sea glass. You see, just like that sea glass, I was once broken, ragged, weathered and tossed about.

However, in that process I was guided and was allowed to follow the flow in which my circumstances led me. Remember in life, there is a purpose for everything and everything has a purpose...even when it is unclear and we ask why. But just know that the outcome is much greater than what we could ever fathom it to be.

Becoming Resilient to Safeguard Your Life

Resiliency, what is that exactly? Well, according to Merriam-Webster, the definition for Resilient – able to become strong, healthy, or successful again after something bad happens. Psychology Today states Resilience – is that ineffable quality that allows some people to be knocked down by life and come back stronger than ever. Another noted definition from the Al Siebert Resiliency Center indicates that Resiliency – a human ability to recover quickly from disruptive change, or misfortune without being overwhelmed or acting in dysfunctional or harmful ways.

So have you ever had a time when everything around you in your life seemed to be falling apart? One day things are fine and the next day all heck breaks loose. Things like your relationships, your finances, your family, your health, your home, your livelihood, and your job, even your sanity has all been shaken to your core to the point of no return. At least, in that moment that's what it seems like as if all is going wrong with no possible end in sight.

Those are times when life hits you with a one two punch feeling like you have just been knocked out by the heavyweight champion of the world. While down for the count, you wonder how did this happen?

Why right now? Who would do this to me? What am I to do now? Where do I go from here? The questions you have keep coming and coming to mind but to no avail without any answers. These are the moments that have the ability to make or break you. These moments can also set the precedence on how you handle the next one.

These are the situations and circumstances that you can't always prepare for because just like that right hook, you didn't see it coming. However, what you can do is learn how to bounce back when it does happen. There is a way to come out unscathed through it all. You see all blows are not a total knock out. Just like that fighter in the ring, you will be dazed but you will get up, go to your corner, regroup, come back out, and keep fighting through it until you become victorious.

So when I think back to the many times I have had setbacks, and major mishaps in my life I had to think what did do that has made me so buoyant today. How have I safeguarded my life to become resilient? Well, I placed my focus on my 5 core areas that I believe has made a significant different in my life. By aligning within these areas over time I allowed myself to be able to bounce back and be better than before.

I created my own personal support system by nurturing my core: spiritual, physical, emotional, mental and social well-being. I gave attention to these 5 core parts within my support system and this has been my solace. I can attest that by putting energy and focus on these elements they continue to build me up, to get me up, and to keep me going through it all. Now it's time for you to do the same.

Remember, if you are brought to it you will be brought through it. Take your setbacks and turn them into comebacks. Safeguard your life, focus on the five and become more resilient than ever!

One Link is All it Takes....

When I think of something being tied down I immediately think of chains. Chains are a series of links connected together meant to keep something bound and restricted to a certain area of confinement. I've noticed we place chains on our pets when we want to contain them. We place chains on our fences when we want to keep them locked. I have even seen where chains were placed on trash cans to keep them from blowing away. Basically, we put chains on anything we want to keep in its place and what we want to protect.

Well, guess what? We also put chains on our problems, our circumstances and even our hearts. We keep them bound to us making sure that our problem, circumstance and heart stays real close to us on purpose. You see if we didn't tie them up we run the risk of being embarrassed, being talked about and being hurt. So when it comes to locking up your property and your heart nothing can get in and nothing can get out.

Let's take for instance your heart, if you are afraid of letting anyone get close to you for fear of getting hurt then your heart is bounded. Love can't come in and love can't come out. If your past pain has led you to live an unfavorable life that you are not happy with then you are bound by your circumstances.

Somethings are beyond your control but you control what you do with it. If there's a situation that you are dealing with and you choose not to seek help to rectify it then you are bound to your problems. Nothing will change and things will remain the same.

The chains are only there because we put them there. We put them there as a sense of security and as a way to protect ourselves. Little do we know that by doing so we actually are causing more damage than good to our overall well-being. Once we realize, that it is up to us whether we stay bounded or not – the process of breaking the chains has already begun.

Like in the song "Break Every Chain" from Tasha Cobbs – a verse she sings repeatedly is "I Hear the Chains Falling" this is confirmation to yourself that the chains have been broken. I can personally relate to keeping myself bound as this was something I have done for years. Afraid to move forward, afraid to make things better, afraid to let anything or anyone in or out. I remember the first time I heard this song it impacted me tremendously where I decided I was ready to let go and let God help me remove these chains.

But I can say that from that moment and through this journey of Magnify Your Essence and discovering my true me has definitely allowed me to break every chain and I can definitely hear my chains falling one by one. I believe that you can also begin to hear your own chains falling all it takes is one link to be broken in order to have them fall. So go ahead and give yourself permission to release yourself from your restraints, the chains that have had you bound for way too long. You deserve to have them be broken. You deserve to be free. Just remember – ONE link is all it takes!

What are some of your Magnified Thoughts?

_____

_____

_____

_____

_____

_____

_____

_____

_____

_____

_____

_____

_____

_____

_____

_____

Carolyn Wilson

_____

_____

_____

_____

_____

_____

_____

_____

_____

_____

_____

_____

_____

_____

_____

_____

_____

_____

_____

_____

❀ Carolyn Wilson

Trail of Nuggets

TDN

(Today's Daily Nuggets)

Magnified Quotes

Overall the next several pages reflect on
each quote and write how each quote
applies to you. Write down what comes
to mind. Then make it your own.
Embrace it…Believe it…Become it!

Believe in your beliefs until it's your truth! ~ M.Y.E.

_____

_____

_____

_____

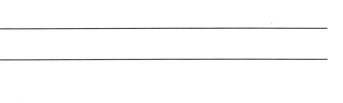

No time like the present…Follow your dreams and watch them transform your life. ~ M.Y.E.

_____

_____

_____

_____

C hoose STRENGTH over Fear...it BECOMES your FAVOR! ~ M.Y.E.

_____

_____

_____

_____

Do great things today that will make a BIG difference tomorrow! ~ M.Y.E.

_____

_____

_____

_____

B e Bold...Be Strong...Find your Voice...then Use it! ~ M.Y.E

_____

_____

_____

_____

t's your time to shine...let your glow be so bright it leads the way! ~ M.Y.E.

_____

_____

_____

_____

Embrace the changes...it's all working out for your good! ~ M.Y.E

_____

_____

_____

_____

E

ndless possibilities happen when you are determined! ~ M.Y.E

_____

_____

_____

_____

Basic rules to live by...Keep it moving...make a difference for you! ~ M.Y.E

What sparks your momentum and where is it taking you? ~ M.Y.E

_____

_____

_____

_____

D ream Big and Believe ~ M.Y.E

_____

_____

_____

_____

Happiness is a choice...What decision have you made for you? ~ M.Y.E.

_____

_____

_____

_____

When you're that focused, that determined...nothing can stop you from blooming! ~ M.Y.E

_____

_____

_____

_____

Make determination the driving force to your destination! ~ M.Y.E

_____

_____

_____

_____

O nly YOU can Make IT happen! ~ M.Y.E

_____

_____

_____

_____

B

elieve the impossible will be possible!
~ M.Y.E

One must believe in their own amazing abilities, gifts and talents. For amazing people end up doing amazing things. ~ M.Y.E

_____

_____

_____

_____

Fearless + Resilience = Powerful

~ M.Y.E

_____

_____

_____

_____

Because I am fearless…I am powerful
~ M.Y.E.

_____

_____

_____

_____

E mbrace the power of a Fearless woman
~ M.Y.E

_____

_____

_____

_____

Your purpose is the gift that keeps on giving! ~ M.Y.E

_____

_____

_____

_____

D

iscover your gift…the world is
waiting. ~ M.Y.E

_____

_____

_____

_____

Take a moment to enjoy and appreciate the little things in life...because what may be little to you might be big to someone else! ~ M.Y.E

_____

_____

_____

_____

Enjoy the little things in life ~ M.Y.E

_____

_____

_____

_____

C elebrate the Journey, the Milestones both great and small including the Pit Stops along the way! ~ M.Y.E

_____

_____

_____

_____

t's not about the destination…it's about the journey that got you there ~ M.Y.E.

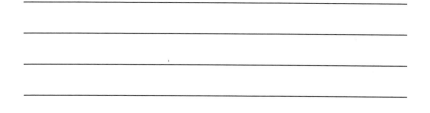

_____

_____

_____

_____

Every day is a blessing worth being acknowledged! ~ M.Y.E

_____

_____

_____

_____

C ount your blessings everyday ~ M.Y.E

_____

_____

_____

_____

T he art of giving back is your greatest masterpiece! ~ M.Y.E

_____

_____

_____

_____

Want more? Give more! ~ M.Y.E.

_____

_____

_____

_____

Do what you love and love what you do…It's just that simple…just do you! ~ M.Y.E

_____

_____

_____

_____

f you can SEE it, and you BELIEVE it, then you WILL ACHIEVE it!!! ~ M.Y.E

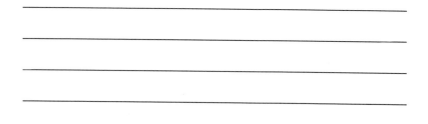

Note to self: If you Remain Dedicated and Stay Focused - Success is Inevitable! ~ M.Y.E

_____

_____

_____

_____

S eize the moment and reach new heights!
~ M.Y.E

I n all that you do...just be you! ~ M.Y.E

_____

_____

_____

_____

S tay Committed in all you do! M.Y.E

_____

_____

_____

_____

Today is the day to do amazing things -
now make it count!!! ~ M.Y.E

_____

_____

_____

_____

Embrace your fierceness...others see you the way you see yourself...now go ahead and ROAR! ~ M.Y.E

_____

_____

_____

_____

A lway be True to You...it's who you are!
~ M.Y.E

_____

_____

_____

_____

S ometimes we need the rocks in the road...they may block us but never stop us...they help us figure out what to do next along our journey! ~ M.Y.E

_____

_____

_____

_____

Don't sweat the SMALL stuff...because it's the little things that makes a BIG difference. ~ M.Y.E

B e bold...Take risk...Venture into the unknown...Just try...You never know it just might be right for you! ~ M.Y.E

_____

_____

_____

_____

Believe in yourself and make your dreams comes true...now go and prove that! ~ M.Y.E

_____

_____

_____

_____

S trength definitely comes from within...embrace it! ~ M.Y.E

_____

_____

_____

_____

H appiness is not a given...it's a choice ~ M.Y.E

_____

_____

_____

_____

You get new opportunities everyday...so why not take advantage of it...Just repeat..."This is going to be my day"..and so it shall be!!! ~ M.Y.E

_____

_____

_____

_____

Be Strong...Be Bold...Be Daring...in order for your light to shine...Let your Essence Be magnified!!! ~ M.Y.E

L ive your life to the fullest...Love the skin your in ~ M.Y.E

A lways pay it forward...no matter how great or small...whether you think you can or cannot...the give back is essential...it's a requirement ~ M.Y.E

_____

_____

_____

_____

L ive your life...embrace your dreams...be happy while doing it. ~ M.Y.E

Carolyn Wilson

New Beginnings can only happen if you allow them to. ~ M.Y.E

_____

_____

_____

_____

L etting go allows for something new...what are you willing to let go of? ~ M.Y.E

_____

_____

_____

_____

am in charge of my own happiness...things and people just add to it ~ M.Y.E

_____

_____

_____

_____

Y ou'll never know what you can do unless you try ~ M.Y.E

_____

_____

_____

_____

C hallenge yourself....What challenges are you willing to conquer? ~ M.Y.E

_____

_____

_____

_____

C hallenge yourself with something you know you could never do and happiness is only a thought away ~ M.Y.E

The power of positive thinking goes along way. You can accomplish so much more when you simply change the way you think. You bring about what you think about. So go on and try it good things are waiting for you! ~ M.Y.E

_____

_____

_____

_____

Dare to Be Different and Unique...simply put Be Amazing in all that you do! ~M.Y.E

f you thought trusting others was hard...how about trusting yourself....guess what both can be done and it all starts with you! ~ M.Y.E

_____

_____

_____

_____

Today will be Terrific! Why because you said so and so it will be! ~ M.Y.E

_____

_____

_____

_____

Change your thoughts…change your life…change the world!!! ~ M.Y.E

_____

_____

_____

_____

am a Woman on the Move!!! Watch me go…Vroom Vroom!!! ~ M.Y.E

_____

_____

_____

_____

What are your dreams? Let's turn them into reality! When? How about NOW! ~ M.Y.E

_____

_____

_____

_____

G ratitude is the best Attitude! Be grateful at all times….and at all times be grateful! ~ M.Y.E

_____

_____

_____

_____

W
hen passion meets purpose + explosion = girl on blazing fire!!!! ~ M.Y.E

_____

_____

_____

_____

Whatever it is you wish to be, whatever it is you wish to do…Be Bold, Be Daring, Be Brave! ~ M.Y.E

_____

_____

_____

_____

Do something that makes you smile...cherish each moment and make every second count. ~ M.Y.E

Happiness is way of life, a mindset a state of being....now go SMILE and be happy! ~ M.Y.E

_____

_____

_____

_____

New Beginnings are like starting a new chapter in the wonderful book of you….a brilliant story! ~ M.Y.E

_____

_____

_____

_____

You are what you think, what you say, what you do, and what you feel. This is your reflection and each day is directed by you! ~ M.Y.E

_____

_____

_____

_____

T his is the life that I choose…one that's unstoppable and courageous!! ~ M.Y.E

et's make the most of your day today. Remember, you are destined for greatness today and beyond. HE wanted you to know that! ~ M.Y.E

_____

_____

_____

_____

Free your soul, Free your mind, Free yourself and live YOUR dream! ~ M.Y.E

oday is beautiful because of my yesterday and because of my tomorrow. Enjoy today, every day and every moment! ~ M.Y.E

_____

_____

_____

_____

Your assignment…In order to be amazing you must DARE and DECLARE to be amazing! ~ M.Y.E

_____

_____

_____

_____

G reatness is in us all….you just have to believe! ~ M.Y.E

When deciding what to wear each morning, put Confidence on...it looks good on you! ~ M.Y.E

_____

_____

_____

_____

M

ove fearlessly into your
Greatness!! ~ M.Y.E

Be purposeful…devote yourself and you will be the creator of great things! ~ M.Y.E

_____

_____

_____

_____

C ontinue to Dream and Shine brightly for everyone to see your beautiful Sparkle!
~ M.Y.E

_____

_____

_____

_____

What Nugget will you leave on the trail?
What will be your own Personal Motto?

Trust it! Acknowledge it! Embrace it!
Be Magnified!

Final Thoughts

It took almost 3 years to finally get the courage to release this book. I'm glad that I did. It is my hope that this book has blessed you and has given you the inspiration, motivation and encouragement that you may need to get through anything. Remember the power lies between you and your thoughts. When you change your thoughts you can change your life.

"Be transformed by the renewal of your mind" Romans 12:2

Feel free to share your Magnified Thoughts with me. - **magnifyyouressence@yahoo.com**

Resources

HOTLINES:

National Sexual Assault Telephone Hotline
800.656.HOPE (4673)

National Domestic Violence Hotline
1-800-799-SAFE (7233)
1-800-787-3224 (TTY)

RESOURCES:

Rape, Abuse & Incest National Network - https://www.rainn.org/
National Domestic Violence Hotline - http://www.thehotline.org/
Women Against Abuse – http://www.womenagainstabuse.org/
Lutheran Settlement House – http://www.lutheransettlement.org/
Woman Organized Against Rape - https://www.woar.org/
Survivors of Incest Anonymous – https://www.siawso.org/
Safe Horizon - https://www.safehorizon.org/

Sources:

https://www.justice.gov/ovw/domestic-violence

https://www.azlyrics.com/lyrics/whitneyhouston/whenyoubelieve.html

https://www.psychologytoday.com/basics/fear

Acknowledgments

None of this wouldn't be possible without the strength given to me by GOD. And, the loving support from my family: my Grandmother Laforest, my wonderful children Russell & Jennifer. My aunt's Asha, Janet, Charlotte, Karen, Terri & Camilla, My Uncle Beanie, my cousins Imani, Holly, Naimah, Lashan, Marcy, Wendy, John, Shardae, Casey, Quinn, Nicole, Melita, Kimberly, Shannon, Fred & Alex, my Pastor Rev. Regina Goodrich, my SIA family, my friends Big Russell, Felicia, Danielle, Scharita, Terri, Ursula, Saniyyah, Stephanie.M, Margaret, Yvonne, Monique, Valerie, Veronica, Lisa Marie, Michelle, Heather, Ma'Sonya, Norma, Gary, Fred.H, my spiritual counselors Milena & Norm, my bffwillas Stephanie.T, my adoptive family Ms. Linda & Mr. Leon, my God-daughter Bryanna, my sorors of Gamma Phi Delta and a host of others who were there willing to sit with me, listen to my story and to help me navigate through a very dark time in my life when I needed help the most.

Thank you all from the bottom of my heart and from the crown of my head to the souls of my feet. I love you all for supporting me through my journey of healing and discovering a new me…a Magnified Me!

About the Author

Carolyn Wilson, The Fearless Magnified Educator, is an empowerment expert who educates, empowers, and inspires women to see and reach their full potential. A survivor of sexual child abuse and domestic violence, this single mom guides women to identify their life's purpose and how to break through their own barriers. She helps them to overcome their number one culprit – FEAR. Carolyn is a master of positive thinking and being able to strategically align your gifts and talents with your purpose. She wants to help you "Magnify Your Essence" through your thoughts, words and deeds. Her aim through writing this book is, to help you discover your true you, to be free and to be magnified. She is a woman on a mission to empower and inspire women in every walk of life. Carolyn is *A Woman on the Move* whose *Essence* has been *Magnified!* Everyday Carolyn strives to make a difference by helping others tap into their boldness and by motivating them personally, professionally, and spiritually. She uses her many gifts and talents in finance, business, leadership, teaching and her own life's experiences to get the task done. She's an educator, a business woman, a motivational speaker, an author, a blogger, and a mentor to many. Carolyn is a strong believer that "to whom much is given, much is required" and that the give back is essential. Through her experience, modesty and transparency she's made herself a living example for others to emulate.

Carolyn devotes her time and talent with outside activities to many non-profits committees and organizations. She holds a MBA from Philadelphia

University, Bachelor of Science Degree from Gwynedd-Mercy University, and an Associate of Science Degree from Community College of Philadelphia. She's a proud member of Gamma Phi Delta Sorority, Inc. Presently she's an Adjunct Professor, a Business Analyst, and a Community Leader. And most importantly, Carolyn is a single mother of two amazing children. She enjoys spending quality time with family and friends and giving back to her community.

Magnify Your Essence™
"journey to discovering the true you"

PO Box 271

Cheltenham, PA 19012

For more information about Magnify Your Essence or to Book Carolyn for your next event visit:

www.magnifyyouressence.wordpress.com

Made in the USA
Middletown, DE
31 August 2018